THE BUSINESS SUCCESS GUIDE TO ALPACAS FARMING

A Complete Insight To Raising, Breeding, Profiting Essential Tips On Care, Nutrition, And Sustainable Practices

RICHMOND HAMILL

© 2024 [RICHMOND HAMILL]. All rights reserved.

Except for brief quotations included in critical reviews and certain other noncommercial uses allowed by copyright law, no part of this book may be reproduced, distributed, or transmitted in any form or by any means, including photocopying, recording, or other electronic or mechanical methods, without the publisher's prior written permission.

Disclaimer

The information presented in this book is based on the author's personal knowledge and understanding of livestock management. The author is not affiliated with any association, company, business, or individual in the livestock industry. All content is provided for informational purposes only and should not be considered as professional advice. Readers are encouraged to seek professional guidance and conduct their own research before making any decisions based on the information contained in this book. The author and publisher disclaim any liability for any adverse effects or consequences resulting from the use of the information contained herein.

TABLE OF CONTENTS

CHAPTER ONE 13
Introduction To Alpaca Farming 13

Overview Of Alpaca Farming 13

History And Origin Of Alpacas 14

Benefits Of Alpaca Farming 16

Understanding Alpaca Breeds 17

Basic Alpaca Terminology 19

    Cria: 19

    Herdsire: 19

    Dam: 19

    Sire: 19

CHAPTER TWO 21
Getting Started With Alpacas 21

Setting Up Your Farm 21

Choosing The Right Location 23

Required Equipment And Supplies 24

Understanding Legal Requirements 25

Initial Investment And Budgeting 26

CHAPTER THREE 29

Selecting And Acquiring Alpacas 29

Choosing The Best Breed For Your Farm 29

Finding Reputable Breeders 30

Evaluating Alpaca Health And Quality 32

The Purchase Process 33

Transporting Your Alpacas 34

CHAPTER FOUR 37

Alpaca Housing And Enclosures 37

Designing The Ideal Shelter 37

Creating Safe And Comfortable Living Spaces 38

Fencing And Security Measures 40

Ventilation And Heating Needs 41

Providing Adequate Space For Grazing...........43

CHAPTER FIVE...45

Feeding And Nutrition..45

Basic Nutritional Needs Of Alpacas 45

Types Of Feed And Supplements.....................47

Creating A Balanced Diet Plan 48

Managing Feeding Schedules...........................49

Hydration And Water Requirements...............51

CHAPTER SIX...53

Health And Veterinary Care..............................53

Routine Health Check-Ups 53

Common Alpaca Diseases And Conditions.....54

Vaccinations And Preventative Care................56

Emergency Care Procedures 57

Establishing A Relationship With A Veterinarian 59

CHAPTER SEVEN..61

Breeding And Reproduction 61

Understanding Alpaca Reproductive Cycles ... 61

Breeding Techniques And Practices 63

Caring For Pregnant Females 64

Neonatal Care For Newborn Cria 66

Weaning And Early Development 67

CHAPTER EIGHT 69

Alpaca Grooming And Maintenance 69

Regular Grooming Routines 69

Handling And Shearing 70

Hoof Care And Maintenance 72

Ear And Eye Care 73

Managing Parasites And External Pests 74

CHAPTER NINE 77

Marketing And Selling Alpaca Products 77

Overview Of Alpaca Fiber Uses 77

Developing A Marketing Strategy 78

Building A Brand And Customer Base 80

Pricing And Sales Techniques 82

CHAPTER TEN 85

Financial Management And Record-Keeping . 85

Tracking Farm Expenses And Income 85

Managing Budgets And Financial Planning 87

Record Keeping For Breeding And Health 88

Tax Considerations And Financial Reporting 90

Evaluating Farm Performance And Growth 91

Frequently Asked Question And Answers. 93

CONCLUSION 99

THE END 103

ABOUT THIS BOOK

"Alpacas Farming" serves as an essential guide for anyone interested in venturing into the rewarding world of alpaca farming. This comprehensive resource offers a detailed overview of alpaca farming, starting with the historical and geographical origins of these unique animals, and explores the numerous benefits they bring to a farming operation. Readers will gain a thorough understanding of alpaca breeds and essential terminology, providing a solid foundation for anyone looking to start or enhance their alpaca farming journey.

This guide delves into the practical aspects of setting up an alpaca farm, including choosing the ideal location, acquiring the necessary equipment and supplies, and understanding the legal requirements. It provides insightful advice on budgeting and initial investments, ensuring that prospective farmers are well-prepared for the financial aspects of establishing their farms.

Selecting and acquiring alpacas is a critical phase covered in depth, from choosing the best breed for specific farming goals to finding reputable breeders and evaluating alpaca health. This book details the purchase process and safe transportation of alpacas, helping new farmers make informed decisions.

Alpaca housing and enclosures are addressed with a focus on designing shelters that ensure safety and comfort. This guide includes practical tips on fencing, security measures, and the necessary considerations for ventilation, heating, and grazing space, ensuring that alpacas have a healthy and secure living environment.

Feeding and nutrition are thoroughly discussed, covering the basics of alpaca dietary needs, types of feed and supplements, and creating balanced diet plans. This book emphasizes the importance of hydration and proper feeding schedules to maintain the health and well-being of the alpacas.

Health and veterinary care are crucial components of successful alpaca farming. This guide provides information on routine health check-ups, common diseases, vaccinations, and emergency care. Establishing a relationship with a veterinarian is highlighted as a key aspect of ongoing farm management.

This guide explores the breeding and reproduction of alpacas, detailing reproductive cycles, breeding practices, and care for pregnant females. It also covers neonatal care and early development, offering valuable insights for those interested in expanding their herd.

Grooming and maintenance are essential for alpaca welfare, and This guide offers comprehensive advice on regular grooming routines, shearing, hoof care, and managing parasites and pests. Proper care of ears and eyes is also discussed, ensuring that alpacas remain in optimal health.

Marketing and selling alpaca products are addressed with a focus on leveraging the unique qualities of alpaca fiber. This guide provides strategies for developing a marketing plan, selling products locally and online, building a brand, and setting effective pricing and sales techniques.

Finally, This book emphasizes the importance of financial management and record-keeping. It offers practical advice on tracking farm expenses and income, managing budgets, maintaining records for breeding and health, and understanding tax considerations. Evaluating farm performance and growth is also discussed, helping farmers make informed decisions to ensure long-term success.

CHAPTER ONE

Introduction To Alpaca Farming

Overview Of Alpaca Farming

Alpaca farming involves raising alpacas primarily for their high-quality fiber, which is used in textiles such as clothing and blankets. The farming process encompasses various activities, including breeding, feeding, and caring for alpacas to ensure their health and productivity. Alpacas are relatively low-maintenance compared to other livestock, making them an appealing choice for small-scale and hobby farmers.

To start alpaca farming, you need to establish a suitable environment for the animals. This involves setting up shelters to protect them from extreme weather conditions and ensuring they have access to clean water and nutritious food.

Alpacas thrive in grassy pastures, so you'll need to manage their grazing areas to maintain healthy pastureland. Regular health check-ups, including vaccinations and deworming, are also essential to prevent diseases.

When beginning, consider the size of your farm and the number of alpacas you wish to keep. It's crucial to plan for adequate space and resources to support their needs. Alpacas are social animals and prefer to be in groups, so it's advisable to start with at least two to prevent loneliness and ensure they have companionship. Additionally, familiarize yourself with local regulations and zoning laws related to alpaca farming.

History And Origin Of Alpacas

Alpacas are native to South America, specifically the Andes Mountains of Peru, Bolivia, and Chile. They have been domesticated for thousands of years, with historical records indicating that they were first bred by the Inca civilization. The Inca people raised alpacas primarily for their fleece, which was highly valued for its softness and warmth.

The alpaca's ancestors, the vicuña and guanaco, were wild animals that roamed the Andean highlands. Over time, these animals were selectively bred for their fiber qualities, resulting in the domesticated alpacas we know today. They were brought to North America in the 1980s, where they have since gained popularity as both livestock and pets due to their gentle nature and high-quality fleece.

Understanding the history of alpacas provides insight into their behavior and needs. Historically, alpacas were used in Andean cultures for their fiber and as pack animals. This background helps modern farmers appreciate the value of maintaining their traditional care practices and ensuring that their environmental and social needs are met.

Benefits Of Alpaca Farming

Alpaca farming offers several advantages for both small and large-scale operations. One of the primary benefits is the production of alpaca fiber, which is known for its softness, warmth, and hypoallergenic properties. Alpaca fleece comes in a variety of natural colors, reducing the need for chemical dyes and making it an attractive option for environmentally conscious consumers.

In addition to fiber production, alpacas are relatively low-maintenance animals compared to other livestock. They have minimal environmental impact due to their efficient grazing habits and gentle hooves, which cause less damage to pastureland. Their manure is an excellent natural fertilizer, which can enhance soil quality and reduce the need for chemical fertilizers.

Alpaca farming also provides an opportunity for diversification in agriculture. Farmers can create niche markets for alpaca products, such as clothing, blankets, and yarn, offering unique items that appeal to consumers. Additionally, alpacas are known for their friendly and curious nature, making them popular among visitors and enhancing agritourism opportunities.

Understanding Alpaca Breeds

Alpacas come in two primary breeds: the Huacaya and the Suri. Huacayas are the most common breed and are characterized by their dense, crimped fleece, which gives them a fluffy appearance. Their fleece has a wool-like texture and is typically shorn once a year. Huacayas are known for their adaptability to various climates and their friendly, social behavior.

The Suri alpaca, on the other hand, has long, silky fleece that grows in distinct, lustrous locks. This breed's fleece is less crimped and requires more frequent grooming to prevent tangling. Suri alpacas are often chosen for their unique fiber characteristics and are less common than Huacayas. They are well-suited to cooler climates and can be more sensitive to heat.

When choosing alpacas for your farm, consider the specific qualities of each breed and how they align with your goals. Huacayas are generally easier to care for and maybe a better choice for beginners. Suri alpacas, while more demanding in terms of grooming, can produce highly desirable fleece for specialized markets. Understanding these breeds will help you make informed decisions about which alpacas are best suited for your farming operation.

Basic Alpaca Terminology

Understanding basic alpaca terminology is crucial for effective communication and management in alpaca farming. Here are some key terms:

Cria: A baby alpaca, typically born after an 11.5-month gestation period. Cria are weaned around 6-8 months of age.

Herdsire: A male alpaca used for breeding. Herds are selected for their superior genetic traits to improve the quality of the offspring.

Dam: The mother alpaca. The term "dam" is used to refer to the female alpaca that has given birth to a cria.

Sire: The father alpaca. The sire contributes to the genetic makeup of the cria and is chosen based on desirable traits.

Fleece: The wool or fiber produced by alpacas. Fleece quality can vary based on breed, age, and genetics.

Familiarizing yourself with these terms will help you better understand the alpaca farming process and communicate effectively with other farmers, breeders, and veterinarians. Knowing the terminology also aids in the proper management of breeding, care, and marketing of alpaca products.

CHAPTER TWO

Getting Started With Alpacas

Setting Up Your Farm

Setting up an alpaca farm begins with creating a suitable environment for these gentle animals. Start by selecting a location that offers adequate space, as alpacas need room to graze and roam. Ideally, you should have at least one acre per three to five alpacas, though more space is beneficial. The land should be well-drained to prevent issues like foot rot and other health problems. Ensure there's access to clean water and that the pasture is free of toxic plants.

Next, construct proper fencing to keep your alpacas secure and contained. Fences should be at least 4 to 5 feet high to prevent them from escaping.

A combination of electric and wire fencing can be effective. Design your pasture layout with separate areas for grazing, shelter, and exercise to promote a healthy lifestyle for your alpacas. Additionally, plan for easy access to feed and hay storage to streamline daily operations.

Consider the climate of your location. Alpacas are generally hardy but thrive in moderate climates. If you live in an area with extreme weather conditions, you will need to provide shelter to protect them from harsh temperatures, wind, and rain. Building a simple three-sided shelter or shed with adequate ventilation can offer protection and comfort. Ensure the shelter is easily accessible for you to clean and manage.

Choosing The Right Location

When choosing the right location for your alpaca farm, evaluate both the land and the surrounding environment. Opt for land with good soil quality and access to water sources, as alpacas require fresh water daily. The site should be away from high-traffic areas and potential hazards, such as busy roads or large predators.

Proximity to veterinary services and alpaca supply stores is also important. Having access to specialized care and resources can make managing your farm easier. Additionally, consider the distance from your home or work, as regular daily visits are necessary to care for your alpacas effectively.

Before finalizing your location, check the local zoning laws and regulations regarding livestock. Some areas have restrictions on the number of animals you can keep or specific requirements for their care. It's crucial to ensure that your chosen location complies with these regulations to avoid future complications.

Required Equipment And Supplies

To manage an alpaca farm effectively, you will need specific equipment and supplies. Basic supplies include feeding troughs, water buckets, and a high-quality hay feeder. Alpacas also require grooming tools such as brushes, clippers, and a hoof-trimming kit. Regular grooming is essential for their health and comfort.

Invest in a first aid kit with basic veterinary supplies for emergencies. This should include items like antiseptics, bandages, and any medications recommended by your vet. Additionally, you'll need a reliable system for waste management to maintain cleanliness and prevent the spread of disease.

Consider investing in a high-quality fence and gate system to ensure the safety of your alpacas. The fencing should be durable and easy to maintain. Also, having a secure and well-organized storage area for feed, hay, and supplies will make daily operations smoother and more efficient.

Understanding Legal Requirements

Before starting your alpaca farm, familiarize yourself with the legal requirements in your area. This includes zoning laws, animal welfare regulations, and any necessary permits or licenses. Contact your local government or agricultural extension office to gather information on the specific requirements for raising alpacas.

You may need to register your farm with local authorities and adhere to regulations regarding animal health and safety.

Some areas require regular inspections or vaccinations for livestock. Ensure you are compliant with these regulations to avoid fines or legal issues.

Additionally, consider insurance coverage for your farm. Liability insurance can protect you in case of accidents or injuries involving your alpacas. Research different insurance options and choose a policy that covers both property and livestock to safeguard your investment.

Initial Investment And Budgeting

Starting an alpaca farm involves an initial investment in land, equipment, and alpacas themselves. Begin by creating a detailed budget that includes costs for land acquisition or rental, fencing, shelter construction, and necessary equipment. Factor in the costs of purchasing alpacas, which can vary based on their quality and lineage.

Ongoing expenses include feed, veterinary care, and maintenance of equipment and facilities. It's essential to budget for these recurring costs to ensure the sustainability of your farm. Keep track of all expenses and income to manage your finances effectively and make informed decisions about your farm's growth and development.

Consider setting aside a contingency fund for unexpected expenses, such as medical emergencies or repairs. Planning for these potential costs will help you maintain smooth operations and avoid financial strain. Regularly review and adjust your budget as needed to ensure your alpaca farm remains a successful and enjoyable venture.

CHAPTER THREE

Selecting And Acquiring Alpacas

Choosing The Best Breed For Your Farm

Selecting the right breed of alpaca is crucial for a successful farming experience. Alpacas are typically classified into two main breeds: Huacaya and Suri. Huacaya alpacas have a dense, crimped fleece that is soft and fluffy, ideal for creating warm, high-quality fiber. They are generally more common and easier to care for, making them a popular choice for beginners. Suri alpacas, on the other hand, have long, silky fleece that hangs in lustrous locks. While they require a bit more maintenance to keep their fleece from matting, their fiber is highly prized for its unique texture and sheen.

When choosing the breed for your farm, consider your primary goals. If your focus is on producing high-quality fleece for spinning or weaving, both breeds can meet this need, but the choice between the two may depend on your preference for fleece type and maintenance. Additionally, think about the climate and environment of your farm. Huacayas are generally more adaptable to varying weather conditions, whereas Suris may need extra care in harsher climates. Understanding the specific characteristics of each breed will help you make an informed decision that aligns with your farming objectives.

Finding Reputable Breeders

Finding a reputable breeder is essential to ensure you acquire healthy and well-bred alpacas. Start by researching local and national alpaca breeders' associations, such as the Alpaca Owners Association

(AOA) in the United States or similar organizations in other countries. These associations often have directories or member lists that include experienced and ethical breeders. Reach out to these breeders to gather information about their practices, the health of their animals, and their breeding programs.

Visit potential breeders in person if possible. This allows you to see the alpacas firsthand, observe their living conditions, and ask detailed questions about their care and breeding practices. Look for breeders who prioritize the health and well-being of their animals, have transparent records, and are willing to provide references from other buyers. A reputable breeder should also be able to provide a detailed history of the alpacas, including vaccinations, health checks, and any genetic testing results.

Evaluating Alpaca Health And Quality

When evaluating alpacas for purchase, focus on their overall health and fleece quality. Healthy alpacas should have bright, clear eyes, clean ears, and a smooth, shiny coat. Check for signs of parasites or skin issues, such as dandruff or sores. The body condition should be neither too thin nor too overweight, and the alpacas should move freely without signs of lameness.

For fleece quality, assess the fineness, crimp, and uniformity of the fiber. The fleece should be dense and well-formed, without excessive matting or breakage. Pay attention to the alpaca's lineage and whether it has won any awards at fiber shows, which can indicate high-quality fleece. Additionally, inquire about the alpaca's genetic background to ensure it does not have any hereditary issues that could impact its health or productivity.

The Purchase Process

The purchase process involves several key steps. Once you've selected the alpacas you wish to buy, negotiate the price with the breeder. Prices can vary based on the alpaca's breed, quality, and pedigree, so be prepared to discuss and possibly negotiate. Ensure that you receive a written contract outlining the terms of the sale, including the purchase price, any warranties or guarantees, and the health status of the alpacas.

Before finalizing the purchase, arrange for a veterinary check to confirm the alpacas' health status. This step can help you avoid any unexpected issues and ensure that the animals are fit for transport. Once the contract is signed and payment is made, discuss the details of the transfer, including any necessary documentation, such as registration papers and health certificates. Keep a copy of all documents for your records.

Transporting Your Alpacas

Transporting alpacas requires careful planning to ensure their safety and well-being. Start by preparing a suitable transport vehicle. Alpacas should be transported in a well-ventilated, enclosed trailer or vehicle that provides ample space for them to stand and lie down comfortably. The trailer should have non-slip flooring and secure partitions to prevent the animals from moving around too much during transit.

Before loading the alpacas, ensure they are calm and accustomed to the process. Practice loading and unloading with them to reduce stress. During transport, provide water and monitor the temperature to keep the environment comfortable.

If the journey is long, plan for rest stops to check on the alpacas and offer them water. Upon arrival at your farm, allow the alpacas some time to acclimate to their new environment and provide them with fresh water, feed, and a clean, safe area to settle into.

CHAPTER FOUR

Alpaca Housing And Enclosures

Designing The Ideal Shelter

Designing a suitable shelter for alpacas is crucial to their health and well-being. The ideal alpaca shelter should protect from extreme weather conditions while allowing for adequate ventilation. Begin by selecting a location that is well-drained and free from flooding. This will prevent water from pooling around the shelter, which can lead to damp conditions detrimental to alpacas' health.

When constructing the shelter, ensure it is spacious enough to accommodate all your alpacas comfortably. A good rule of thumb is to allow at least 30 square feet per alpaca in the shelter area. Use durable materials like treated wood or metal to build the structure. The shelter should have a solid roof to keep rain and snow out, and the walls should be high enough to prevent drafty conditions. For the floor, consider using gravel or concrete covered with straw or hay to provide a dry, comfortable surface.

The entrance to the shelter should be large enough to allow easy access but not so wide that it compromises the interior temperature. Ideally, place the entrance away from prevailing winds. Adding a small overhang or awning above the entrance can also help keep the area dry. Proper lighting is important too; natural light through windows or skylights helps maintain a healthy environment and keeps the shelter bright and inviting.

Creating Safe And Comfortable Living Spaces

To create a safe and comfortable living space for alpacas, focus on the bedding and interior layout. Use straw, hay, or wood shavings as bedding material, as these options are absorbent and help keep the area clean. Regularly clean the bedding and replace it as needed to prevent the buildup of waste and maintain hygiene. Providing soft, clean bedding not only helps in temperature regulation but also minimizes the risk of injuries.

Arrange the interior of the shelter to allow for easy movement and access to feed and water. Install feed troughs and water containers at a convenient height to avoid spillage and ensure alpacas can reach their food and water without difficulty. Ensure that these feeding and watering stations are easily accessible from different areas within the shelter to reduce competition and stress among the animals.

Adding some enrichment items such as hanging toys or objects to chew on can keep the alpacas entertained and reduce boredom. However, make sure that these items are safe and cannot cause injuries.

Additionally, installing a sturdy door or gate to control access to the shelter can help manage interactions between alpacas and protect them from potential predators.

Fencing And Security Measures

Fencing is an essential component of alpaca enclosures, providing security and preventing the animals from wandering off. Use strong, high-quality fencing materials that are at least 4 to 5 feet high. Electric fencing is a popular option as it deters predators and keeps alpacas securely contained. However, ensure that the electric fence is properly maintained and tested regularly.

The fence should be buried at least 12 inches below the ground to prevent alpacas from digging under it. Additionally, installing fencing that is closely spaced at the bottom can prevent smaller animals from squeezing through.

Regularly inspect the fence for signs of wear and tear and promptly repair any damage to maintain its effectiveness.

For added security, consider installing motion-activated lights or cameras around the perimeter of the enclosure. These can help deter nocturnal predators and alert you to any unusual activity. Always ensure that gates are securely latched and check them regularly to ensure they are in good working order.

Ventilation And Heating Needs

Proper ventilation is vital for maintaining a healthy environment within the alpaca shelter. Good ventilation helps remove excess moisture and prevents the buildup of ammonia from urine, which can lead to respiratory issues. Incorporate vents or windows into the shelter design to allow for cross-ventilation. These should be adjustable so you can control airflow depending on the weather conditions.

In colder climates, consider installing a heating system to keep the shelter warm during the winter months. However, be cautious with heating devices to avoid fire hazards. Electric heaters or infrared lamps can be effective, but ensure they are placed safely and cannot be knocked over. Alternatively, you can insulate the shelter to retain heat more efficiently, using materials like foam boards or reflective insulation.

In warmer climates, it's important to prevent overheating. Install fans or use shade cloths to keep the shelter cool and ensure there is always a shaded area available. Providing plenty of fresh, cool water and ensuring that the alpacas have access to shade at all times can also help regulate their body temperature and keep them comfortable.

Providing Adequate Space For Grazing

Adequate grazing space is crucial for the well-being of alpacas, as they require ample room to roam and graze. Allocate a minimum of 200 square feet per alpaca for outdoor grazing areas. The grazing area should be securely fenced to prevent the alpacas from straying and to keep them safe from predators.

Regularly rotate grazing areas to prevent overgrazing and allow the pasture to recover. This practice helps maintain the health of the pasture and provides the alpacas with a variety of plants to consume. Additionally, supplement their diet with hay or other feed options if the pasture does not provide sufficient nutrients.

Ensure that the grazing area has access to clean, fresh water at all times. Installing a water trough or automatic watered can make it easier to provide this essential resource. Regularly inspect the grazing area for any hazards, such as sharp objects or toxic plants, and address any issues promptly to ensure a safe and enjoyable environment for your alpacas.

CHAPTER FIVE

Feeding And Nutrition

Basic Nutritional Needs Of Alpacas

Alpacas are herbivores with specific dietary needs essential for their health and well-being. Their basic nutritional needs primarily include high-fiber forages, a balanced mix of proteins, carbohydrates, and fats, as well as essential vitamins and minerals. The foundation of an alpaca's diet is hay, particularly high-quality grass hay or alfalfa, which provides the necessary fiber to support their digestive system. Fiber aids in proper digestion and prevents issues such as colic or digestive disturbances.

In addition to forage, alpacas need a source of protein to maintain muscle mass and overall health. Young, growing alpacas and pregnant or lactating females have higher protein requirements than mature, non-breeding adults. Protein-rich supplements like alfalfa hay or protein pellets can help meet these needs. Alpacas also require carbohydrates for energy, which are provided by their forage and sometimes supplemented with grains. However, grains should be introduced cautiously to avoid digestive problems.

Minerals and vitamins are crucial for maintaining a balanced diet. Alpacas need minerals like calcium, phosphorus, and magnesium, which can be provided through a mineral supplement or a specially formulated alpaca feed. Vitamins A, D, and E are also important, and their needs can be met through a combination of quality feed and supplements. Regular monitoring and adjustments to their diet are essential to ensure all nutritional requirements are met.

Types Of Feed And Supplements

Choosing the right feed and supplements is vital for the health and productivity of alpacas. The primary feed types include hay, pasture, and grain. Hay is the staple food, with grass hay being a common choice due to its high fiber content. Alfalfa hay is another option, particularly useful for pregnant or lactating females and young alpacas due to its higher protein content.

Pasture grazing is beneficial as it provides fresh forage and natural enrichment. However, the quality of pasture can vary, so it's essential to monitor the nutritional content of the grass and supplement as needed. Grains are used sparingly and should be introduced gradually to avoid digestive upset.

Supplements are used to address specific dietary deficiencies. For example, mineral supplements provide essential nutrients that may be lacking in the forage. Vitamin supplements can support overall health and immune function. Protein supplements, such as soybean meal or alfalfa pellets, can be used for alpacas with increased protein needs. Always choose high-quality, species-appropriate supplements and consult with a veterinarian or animal nutritionist to ensure the proper balance of nutrients.

Creating A Balanced Diet Plan

A balanced diet plan for alpacas involves calculating their nutritional needs based on their age, weight, and reproductive status. Start by assessing their current diet and determining if it meets their fiber, protein, carbohydrate, vitamin, and mineral requirements. This can be done by analyzing the nutritional content of their forage and feed.

To create a balanced diet plan, ensure that the majority of their diet comes from high-fiber forage like grass or alfalfa hay. Supplements should be used to fill any nutritional gaps. For example, if the hay is low in protein, consider adding a protein supplement. If the alpacas are grazing on pasture, supplement their diet with minerals and vitamins if needed.

Regularly monitor your alpacas' body condition and health to adjust their diet as necessary. Weighing the feed and keeping detailed records of their intake can help in making accurate adjustments. Periodic consultations with a veterinarian or nutritionist can provide guidance and help optimize their diet plan to meet changing needs throughout their lifecycle.

Managing Feeding Schedules

Effective feeding schedules help ensure alpacas receive consistent nutrition and maintain their health. Establish a routine for feeding times, ideally providing hay at least twice a day.

Alpacas thrive on routine, so feeding them at the same times each day helps regulate their digestive systems and prevents stress.

When feeding supplements or grains, introduce them gradually and monitor how alpacas respond to avoid digestive issues. For alpacas on pasture, make sure they have access to fresh forage throughout the day, and supplement with hay or other feed as necessary, especially during winter or times of poor pasture growth.

Keep track of each alpaca's individual needs, as their requirements may vary based on factors like age, pregnancy, or lactation. Adjust the feeding schedule as needed to accommodate these changes. Using feeding records and adjusting portions based on body condition and activity level will help maintain their health and prevent overfeeding or underfeeding.

Hydration And Water Requirements

Hydration is crucial for alpacas' health, as they need a consistent supply of clean, fresh water. On average, an adult alpaca will drink between 2 to 5 gallons of water per day, depending on factors such as their diet, size, and environmental conditions. Water consumption can increase during hot weather or when they are consuming dry feed.

Provide access to water at all times, and ensure that it is clean and free from contaminants. Water troughs or buckets should be cleaned regularly to prevent algae growth and contamination. In colder weather, use heated waterers to prevent freezing and ensure that water remains available.

Monitor your alpacas' water intake, as changes in consumption can indicate health issues such as dehydration or kidney problems.

Always provide additional water sources when changing their diet or during periods of high activity. Proper hydration supports digestion, nutrient absorption, and overall well-being, making it a key component of their care regimen.

CHAPTER SIX

Health And Veterinary Care

Routine Health Check-Ups

Routine health check-ups for alpacas are essential to maintaining their overall well-being and ensuring early detection of any potential health issues. A comprehensive health check involves a series of regular examinations by a qualified veterinarian. Typically, these check-ups should be scheduled every 6 to 12 months, depending on the alpaca's age, health status, and any specific concerns.

During a routine health check-up, the veterinarian will perform a thorough physical examination of the alpaca. This includes checking the alpaca's weight, body condition, and vital signs such as heart rate, respiratory rate, and temperature.

The veterinarian will also examine the alpaca's coat and skin for any signs of parasites or infections. Additionally, the mouth, teeth, and hooves will be inspected for any abnormalities or issues that may require attention.

Routine health check-ups also involve preventive measures such as dental care, hoof trimming, and fecal exams to check for internal parasites. Regular monitoring and management of these aspects are crucial for keeping alpacas healthy and comfortable. Establishing a consistent schedule for these check-ups will help ensure that any issues are identified and addressed promptly, minimizing the risk of more serious health problems.

Common Alpaca Diseases And Conditions

Alpacas are generally hardy animals, but they can be susceptible to certain diseases and conditions. Understanding these common issues is key to effective management and prevention. Some of the most prevalent conditions in alpacas include internal parasites, respiratory infections, and gastrointestinal issues.

Internal parasites such as worms and protozoa can cause a range of health problems, including weight loss, poor coat condition, and diarrhea. Regular deworming and fecal exams can help manage and prevent these issues. Respiratory infections, often caused by bacteria or viruses, can lead to symptoms like coughing, nasal discharge, and difficulty breathing. Good ventilation in alpaca shelters and prompt treatment with appropriate antibiotics can help manage respiratory problems.

Gastrointestinal issues, such as colic or bloat, are also common in alpacas. These can result from dietary changes, ingesting foreign objects, or other factors. Ensuring a balanced diet and monitoring for signs of distress can help prevent and address gastrointestinal problems. It's important to familiarize yourself with the symptoms of these conditions and seek veterinary advice promptly to prevent complications.

Vaccinations And Preventative Care

Vaccinations are a crucial part of preventive care for alpacas, helping to protect them from various infectious diseases. The vaccination schedule for alpacas typically includes vaccines for diseases such as clostridial infections, pneumonia, and tetanus. Your veterinarian can provide a recommended vaccination schedule based on your alpaca's age, health status, and local disease risks.

In addition to vaccinations, preventive care for alpacas includes regular deworming to control internal parasites and external parasite management to address issues such as lice and mites.

Preventive dental care is also important, as dental problems can impact an alpaca's ability to eat and overall health. Regular hoof trimming is essential to prevent lameness and other hoof-related issues.

Proper nutrition and sanitation practices are integral to preventive care. Providing a balanced diet tailored to the specific needs of alpacas and maintaining clean living conditions can help prevent many health problems. Regular monitoring of your alpacas' health and seeking veterinary advice when needed will ensure they remain healthy and thriving.

Emergency Care Procedures

In the event of a health emergency, having a clear understanding of emergency care procedures is crucial for the well-being of your alpacas. Common emergencies may include injury, severe illness, or sudden changes in behavior or health status.

If an alpaca is injured, it's important to assess the severity of the injury and provide initial first aid if possible. This may involve cleaning and bandaging wounds, stabilizing fractures, or providing supportive care. In cases of severe illness, such as respiratory distress or signs of shock, prompt veterinary intervention is essential. Keeping a first aid kit specifically for alpacas and having a plan in place for emergencies will help ensure a quick response.

Maintaining contact information for your veterinarian and knowing their availability for emergencies is vital. Additionally, having a transport plan for getting an alpaca to a veterinary clinic quickly can make a significant difference in the outcome of an emergency. Regularly reviewing and practicing emergency procedures will help you be prepared to handle any unexpected health issues effectively.

Establishing A Relationship With A Veterinarian

Establishing a strong relationship with a veterinarian is key to effective alpaca care. Finding a veterinarian with experience in treating alpacas and developing a good working relationship can greatly benefit your herd's health.

Start by researching local veterinarians who specialize in large or exotic animals, specifically alpacas. Schedule an initial consultation to discuss your alpacas' health needs, vaccination schedules, and any specific concerns you may have. Building a rapport with your veterinarian and ensuring they understand your goals and expectations will facilitate better communication and care.

Regularly updating your veterinarian on any changes in your alpacas' health and maintaining open communication will help address any issues promptly. Additionally, involving your veterinarian in planning preventive care and health management strategies will ensure that your alpacas receive the best possible care. Establishing this ongoing partnership will be invaluable in maintaining the health and well-being of your alpaca herd.

CHAPTER SEVEN

Breeding And Reproduction

Understanding Alpaca Reproductive Cycles

Alpacas have a unique reproductive cycle that is essential for successful breeding. Their reproductive cycle is classified as seasonal, meaning they tend to breed during specific times of the year. Female alpacas, or hembras, exhibit an estrous cycle approximately every 17 days, which lasts for about 24 hours. This period of receptivity is known as "heat" or estrus, where they are fertile and capable of conceiving. Recognizing this cycle is crucial for timing breeding effectively.

The primary signs of estrus in alpacas include increased vocalization, a higher level of activity, and a noticeable change in behavior, such as a heightened interest in males. During this period, the female will exhibit a "sitting" posture, called "Lordosis," where she lowers her front end and elevates her hindquarters. Observing these behavioral cues helps in determining the optimal time for mating.

To ensure successful mating, it is recommended to monitor the female closely for signs of estrus and have a male alpaca, or macho, available for breeding. In the absence of natural mating, artificial insemination can be considered, though it requires specialized knowledge and facilities. Understanding these cycles and signs will streamline the breeding process and enhance the likelihood of successful reproduction.

Breeding Techniques And Practices

When it comes to breeding alpacas, there are several techniques to consider. The most traditional method is natural mating, where a male and female are introduced under supervised conditions. This approach relies on the instincts and behaviors of alpacas, which can lead to a successful mating if the female is in heat and the male is experienced.

For those interested in artificial insemination (AI), it's a viable alternative to natural mating. AI involves collecting semen from a male alpaca and then inseminating the female using a specialized technique. This method requires precise timing to match the female's estrus cycle and the use of an AI protocol. Successful AI can result in improved genetics and broader genetic diversity in your herd.

Additionally, embryo transfer is another advanced breeding technique. This involves fertilizing an egg in a laboratory setting and then transferring the embryo into a recipient female. This method is more complex and costly but allows for the propagation of desirable genetic traits and can be used to enhance herd quality. Regardless of the technique chosen, ensuring proper health and nutrition of both the male and female alpacas is crucial for successful breeding outcomes.

Caring For Pregnant Females

Once a female alpaca is confirmed pregnant, providing proper care throughout her gestation period is essential. Alpaca pregnancies last about 11.5 months or 335 days, and during this time, the pregnant female, or dam, should receive adequate nutrition and medical care. A well-balanced diet, rich in essential nutrients and vitamins, supports the health of both the dam and the developing cria (baby alpaca).

Regular veterinary check-ups are important to monitor the health of the pregnant female and address any potential issues. Common health concerns during pregnancy include parasitic infections and nutritional deficiencies. Ensuring the dam has access to fresh water and a comfortable living environment is also crucial. Providing a clean, dry, and quiet area for the dam to give birth helps reduce stress and complications during labor.

As the due date approaches, it is beneficial to observe the dam for signs of impending labor, such as udder development and behavioral changes. Preparing a birthing area with clean bedding and necessary supplies will facilitate a smoother birthing process. Having a plan in place for any potential emergencies or complications can also ensure that the dam and newborn cria receive timely and effective care.

Neonatal Care For Newborn Cria

After the birth of a cria, immediate care is crucial for ensuring the newborn's health and well-being. The first step is to ensure the cria begins nursing within the first few hours of birth. Colostrum, the first milk produced by the dam, is rich in antibodies and essential for the cria's immune system development. If the dam is unable to nurse the cria, alternative methods such as bottle feeding with a suitable replacement may be necessary.

The cria should be monitored closely for signs of health issues, such as difficulty breathing or lack of movement. Regular checks on the cria's temperature, hydration, and overall condition are important. Providing a warm, dry environment helps maintain the cria's body temperature, as newborns are susceptible to cold stress.

Additionally, establishing a routine for vaccinations and deworming, as recommended by a veterinarian, is important for preventing diseases and promoting long-term health. Ensuring the cria receives socialization and interaction with other alpacas will help with its emotional and psychological development. Early handling and gentle care can contribute to a well-adjusted and healthy young alpaca.

Weaning And Early Development

Weaning is a critical phase in the development of a cria and involves transitioning from a milk-based diet to solid food. Typically, weaning occurs between 6 to 8 months of age, though the exact timing can vary depending on the cria's growth and development.

Gradual introduction to solid foods, such as high-quality hay and specially formulated alpaca feed, helps ease the transition.

During the weaning process, monitoring the cria's weight and health is essential. Ensuring that the cria is consuming sufficient nutrients and maintaining a healthy body condition is crucial. Providing supplemental feed and minerals can support the cria's growth and development during this transition period.

Social interaction with other alpacas and proper handling are important for the cria's behavioral development. Introducing the cria to a herd environment allows for natural socialization and helps build confidence and social skills. Regular health check-ups and vaccinations, as well as continued attention to diet and care, will set the foundation for a healthy and well-adjusted adult alpaca.

CHAPTER EIGHT

Alpaca Grooming And Maintenance

Regular Grooming Routines

Grooming alpacas is a vital part of their overall health and well-being. Regular grooming helps maintain the quality of their fleece, keeps their skin healthy, and allows for early detection of any potential health issues. Begin with brushing your alpaca at least once a week to remove loose fleece, dirt, and debris. Use a slicker brush or a curry comb to loosen and remove tangles and mats from their fleece. Make sure to groom in a calm environment to help your alpaca feel relaxed and cooperative.

In addition to brushing, alpacas need regular checks for their nails and fleece. Trim their toenails every 6 to 8 weeks to prevent overgrowth and potential foot problems. Be careful not to cut too short, as this can cause bleeding. Also, monitor the condition of their fleece; if it becomes matted or excessively dirty, more frequent grooming might be necessary.

Hydration and proper diet also contribute to maintaining healthy fleece. Ensure your alpacas have access to clean, fresh water at all times and provide a balanced diet rich in vitamins and minerals. This will help in keeping their fleece in top condition, reducing the amount of grooming required.

Handling And Shearing

Handling alpacas effectively is essential for their comfort and safety during grooming and shearing. Begin by desensitizing your alpaca to human contact. Spend time walking them on a lead, petting them, and speaking softly to get them used to handling. Positive reinforcement with treats can help create a more cooperative behavior.

Shearing is an annual necessity to prevent overheating and to keep their fleece manageable. It's typically done in the spring, before the hot summer months. To shear an alpaca, first, ensure the animal is calm and properly restrained. Many farmers use a shearing table or harness to secure the alpaca in place. Use professional shears or clippers to carefully remove the fleece, starting from the back and working your way toward the front. Make sure to avoid cutting into the skin and take your time to ensure a smooth, even cut.

After shearing, check for any cuts or nicks and treat them with antiseptic if necessary. The fleece can be collected and prepared for processing. Regular shearing not only keeps your alpacas comfortable but also helps maintain the quality of their fleece, which can be sold or used for various products.

Hoof Care And Maintenance

Proper hoof care is crucial for the overall health and mobility of your alpacas. Alpacas have soft, padded feet that require regular trimming to prevent overgrowth and associated problems. Check their hooves every 6 to 8 weeks for signs of overgrowth or damage. Use a hoof trimmer to carefully trim the excess growth. Be cautious not to cut into the quick, which is the sensitive part of the hoof, as this can cause pain and bleeding.

If you notice any abnormalities, such as cracks or infections, address them promptly. Cracks can be treated with specialized hoof dressings, and infections may require veterinary attention. Keeping the alpaca's living area clean and dry will also help prevent hoof problems.

Regular walking on different surfaces, such as gravel or grass, can help naturally wear down their hooves and keep them in good condition. Ensure their living environment is not overly wet or muddy, as this can lead to hoof problems and infections.

Ear And Eye Care

Maintaining clean ears and eyes is essential for your alpaca's overall health. Check their ears regularly for signs of debris, parasites, or infections. Gently clean the outer part of their ears with a damp cloth if needed, and consult a vet if you notice any persistent problems such as excessive wax or discharge.

Eye care is also important. Inspect their eyes regularly for signs of redness, discharge, or cloudiness, which could indicate infections or other health issues. Clean around the eyes with a soft, damp cloth to remove any crust or debris. If you notice any abnormalities or changes in their vision, seek veterinary advice promptly.

In addition to regular checks, protect their eyes from dust and debris by providing a clean and dust-free environment. For years, ensure that the area where they are housed is free from excessive insects and parasites that can cause discomfort or infections.

Managing Parasites And External Pests

Managing parasites and external pests is a critical aspect of alpaca care. Regularly check your alpacas for signs of pests such as lice, mites, and fleas. Use a fine-toothed comb to check for external parasites in their fleece and on their skin. If pests are detected, consult with a veterinarian for appropriate treatment options.

Implementing a regular deworming schedule can help manage internal parasites. Your vet can recommend the best deworming products and schedule based on your alpacas' specific needs. Ensure that you follow the dosage instructions carefully to avoid under or over-treatment.

Maintaining a clean living environment is also crucial in preventing pest infestations. Regularly clean and disinfect their shelter and bedding, and manage the pasture to minimize pest habitats. Providing a dust-free area and using pest repellents as recommended by your vet can further help in managing external pests and keeping your alpacas healthy.

CHAPTER NINE

Marketing And Selling Alpaca Products

Overview Of Alpaca Fiber Uses

Alpaca fiber is renowned for its luxurious texture and versatility, making it a prized material in the textile industry. This natural fiber comes in a range of colors, from white and black to various shades of brown and gray, allowing for a rich palette of products. The fiber is highly valued for its softness, warmth, and durability, making it ideal for a range of garments and accessories. Common products made from alpaca fiber include sweaters, scarves, socks, and blankets. Each product benefits from the fiber's natural hypoallergenic properties, as it does not contain lanolin, which can irritate sensitive individuals.

To effectively use alpaca fiber, it must first be processed. This involves washing the raw fleece to remove any dirt or grease, followed by carding to separate and align the fibers. The cleaned and carded fiber can then be spun into yarn or blended with other fibers for different textures and strengths. The yarn is then dyed and woven or knitted into finished products. Understanding these uses and the processing steps is essential for anyone looking to market alpaca products effectively, as it ensures that the quality of the final product meets consumer expectations.

Developing A Marketing Strategy

Creating a successful marketing strategy for alpaca products involves understanding your target market, differentiating your products, and setting clear goals. Begin by identifying your target audience, which may include individuals interested in sustainable fashion, high-quality textiles, or luxury goods. Research their preferences and purchasing behaviors to tailor your marketing efforts effectively.

Next, differentiate your alpaca products from competitors by highlighting unique selling points, such as the superior quality of your fiber, the sustainability of your farming practices, or the craftsmanship of your products. Develop a brand story that resonates with your audience and emphasizes the benefits of alpaca fiber. Setting clear, measurable goals—such as increasing online sales by a certain percentage or expanding your customer base—will help you track progress and adjust your strategy as needed.

A comprehensive marketing strategy should include both online and offline components. Utilize social media platforms to engage with potential customers, share the story behind your products, and showcase the quality and versatility of your alpaca items.

Consider partnerships with influencers or bloggers who can help promote your products. Additionally, attend trade shows or local markets to build face-to-face relationships with potential buyers and gain valuable feedback.

Building A Brand And Customer Base

Building a strong brand and a loyal customer base involves creating a consistent and memorable identity for your alpaca products. Start by developing a compelling brand name, logo, and tagline that reflects the essence of your products and appeals to your target audience. Ensure that all your marketing materials, including packaging and promotional content, maintain a cohesive look and message.

Engage with your customers through exceptional service and a strong online presence. Respond promptly to inquiries, provide detailed information about your products, and offer personalized recommendations. Consider creating a customer loyalty program or offering special promotions to encourage repeat purchases. Collect and showcase customer reviews and testimonials to build trust and credibility.

Networking and community involvement can also help strengthen your brand. Partner with other local businesses or artisans to cross-promote products and participate in joint events. Share your knowledge and passion for alpaca farming through blog posts, workshops, or community talks to position yourself as an expert in the field. This approach not only attracts customers but also fosters a sense of connection and loyalty to your brand.

Pricing And Sales Techniques

Setting the right price for your alpaca products involves considering factors such as production costs, market demand, and competitive pricing. Calculate the cost of materials, labor, and overheads to determine a base price that covers expenses and ensures profitability. Research the pricing of similar products in the market to position your items competitively while reflecting the quality and uniqueness of your offerings.

Sales techniques play a crucial role in converting potential customers into buyers. Use persuasive language and highlight the benefits and features of your alpaca products in your sales pitches. Offer limited-time promotions or discounts to create a sense of urgency and encourage immediate purchases. Providing excellent customer service and ensuring a smooth purchasing process will enhance the overall buying experience and foster customer satisfaction.

Additionally, consider bundling products or offering value-added services, such as custom orders or gift wrapping, to increase perceived value and attract more customers. Regularly review your pricing strategy and sales techniques based on customer feedback and market trends to continuously improve and adapt your approach for optimal results.

CHAPTER TEN

Financial Management And Record-Keeping

Tracking Farm Expenses And Income

Tracking farm expenses and income is crucial for maintaining the financial health of an alpaca farm. To effectively manage this, start by setting up a detailed accounting system. Use software like QuickBooks or a simple spreadsheet to record all financial transactions. Begin with categorizing your expenses into sections such as feed, veterinary care, equipment, labor, and utilities. This will help you see where your money is going and identify any areas where you can cut costs.

For income tracking, record all revenue from the sale of alpacas, fiber, and any other farm products. Keep detailed records of each transaction, including dates, amounts, and sources. It's helpful to create invoices for sales to maintain accurate records and ensure you receive payment promptly. Regularly reconcile your records with bank statements to ensure accuracy and catch any discrepancies early.

Additionally, maintain a financial logbook where you can track daily expenses and income. This hands-on approach complements digital records and provides a quick reference for daily transactions. By keeping consistent and detailed records, you will be able to monitor your farm's profitability and make informed decisions about future investments or adjustments.

Managing Budgets And Financial Planning

Creating and managing a budget is essential for the successful operation of an alpaca farm. Start by estimating your annual income and expenses. Consider all potential sources of revenue, such as sales of alpaca fiber, breeding services, and any other products or services you offer. On the expense side, include feed, healthcare, facility maintenance, and any other operational costs.

Once you have a comprehensive list, allocate a portion of your income to each expense category. It's beneficial to set aside funds for unexpected costs, such as emergency veterinary care or repairs. Review your budget regularly and adjust it as necessary based on actual income and expenses. This proactive approach will help you avoid financial surprises and keep your farm running smoothly.

Financial planning should also include long-term goals. Consider future investments in infrastructure, equipment, or expansion of your alpaca herd. Develop a savings plan to fund these goals without straining your current budget. Consulting with a financial advisor who specializes in agricultural businesses can provide additional insights and strategies for managing your farm's finances effectively.

Record Keeping For Breeding And Health

Accurate record-keeping is vital for managing the breeding and health of your alpacas. Start by creating individual health and breeding profiles for each alpaca. Include details such as birth dates, breeding history, vaccinations, and any health issues or treatments.

This information will help you make informed decisions about breeding pairs and monitor the overall health of your herd.

For breeding records, document each mating, including dates, sire and dam information, and the outcomes. Track pregnancies, births, and cria (baby alpaca) development closely. This helps you identify successful breeding practices and ensure the well-being of both the mothers and their offspring.

Use a health log to record any veterinary visits, medications administered, and other health-related activities. Keeping detailed records allows you to spot patterns, such as recurring health issues, and address them proactively. Regularly review these records to ensure that your alpacas are receiving the best possible care and that your breeding program is on track.

Tax Considerations And Financial Reporting

Understanding tax considerations is essential for managing your alpaca farm's finances. Keep thorough records of all income and expenses throughout the year to simplify tax reporting. Familiarize yourself with the tax deductions available to agricultural businesses, such as equipment purchases, feed, and veterinary care. Consulting with a tax professional experienced in farm tax laws can help you maximize deductions and ensure compliance.

When it comes to financial reporting, maintain accurate and up-to-date records of your farm's financial transactions. Prepare financial statements, including profit and loss statements and balance sheets, to provide a clear overview of your farm's financial status. These reports are crucial for tax filing and assessing your farm's profitability.

Additionally, regularly review your financial performance to identify trends and areas for improvement. Financial reporting helps you understand how well your farm is performing and whether you need to adjust your strategies or budget. Staying organized and proactive with your financial records and reporting will support the long-term success of your alpaca farm.

Evaluating Farm Performance And Growth

Evaluating your farm's performance and growth involves assessing various financial and operational metrics. Start by analyzing your profit margins and overall financial health. Compare your actual income and expenses against your budget to determine if you are meeting your financial goals. Regularly review key performance indicators such as revenue per alpaca, cost of feed, and veterinary expenses.

Additionally, evaluate your farm's growth by tracking changes in herd size, productivity, and sales. Analyze trends in breeding success, fiber quality, and market demand for your products. This information will help you identify areas of success and those needing improvement.

To foster growth, set clear objectives, and create actionable plans. For instance, if you notice a high demand for alpaca fiber, consider investing in additional processing equipment or expanding your marketing efforts. Regular performance evaluations allow you to make data-driven decisions and adapt your strategies to achieve sustainable growth and profitability for your alpaca farm.

Frequently Asked Question And Answers.

What are alpacas?

Answer: Alpacas are domesticated South American camelids, similar in appearance to llamas but smaller. They are raised primarily for their fiber, which is soft and hypoallergenic.

How do alpacas differ from llamas?

Answer: While both are camelids, alpacas are smaller, have finer fleece, and are primarily raised for their fiber. Llamas are larger, used for packing, and have coarser wool.

What do alpacas eat?

Answer: Alpacas are herbivores and primarily graze on grasses, hay, and some types of grains. They require a balanced diet to maintain their health and wool quality.

How much space do alpacas need?

Answer: Each alpaca needs about 1-2 acres of pasture. They also need shelter to protect them from extreme weather conditions.

What kind of shelter do alpacas need?

Answer: Alpacas need a shelter that protects them from rain, wind, and extreme temperatures. A simple three-sided shed or barn is usually sufficient.

How often should alpacas be sheared?

Answer: Alpacas should be sheared once a year, usually in the spring, to prevent overheating and to harvest their fiber.

Are alpacas easy to handle?

Answer: Generally, alpacas are gentle and easy to handle. However, regular handling and socialization are important for maintaining their docility.

How can you tell if an alpaca is sick?

Answer: Signs of illness in alpacas include changes in appetite, lethargy, abnormal feces, coughing, or unusual behavior. Regular health checks are crucial for early detection.

Do alpacas require vaccinations?

Answer: Yes, alpacas should be vaccinated against common diseases such as clostridial diseases, rabies, and possibly others depending on their environment and local regulations.

How long is the gestation period for alpacas?

Answer: The gestation period for alpacas is approximately 11.5 months or around 335 days.

What is a cria?

Answer: A cria is a baby alpaca. They are born after a gestation period and typically weigh between 15-20 pounds.

When can a cria be weaned?

Answer: Crias are usually weaned between 6-12 months of age, depending on their growth and development.

How often do alpacas need their feet trimmed?

Answer: Alpacas generally need their feet trimmed every 6-8 weeks to prevent overgrowth and related issues.

Can alpacas live alone?

Answer: Alpacas are herd animals and should be kept with at least one other alpaca. Living alone can lead to stress and behavioral issues.

What kind of fencing is best for alpacas?

Answer: Alpacas need secure fencing to prevent escapes and protect them from predators. Fencing should be at least 4-5 feet high and made of sturdy materials.

Do alpacas need any special care during winter?

Answer: Alpacas have a natural fleece that insulates them against cold weather. However, they need proper shelter to protect them from wet conditions and strong winds.

How can I start alpaca farming?

Answer: Starting alpaca farming involves researching local regulations, securing land and facilities, purchasing alpacas from reputable breeders, and learning about their care and management.

How do I breed alpacas?

Answer: Breeding alpacas involves selecting healthy breeding pairs, understanding their reproductive cycles, and managing mating. It's advisable to consult with experienced breeders for guidance.

What are the primary uses for alpaca fiber?

Answer: Alpaca fiber is used for making clothing, blankets, and other textiles. It is prized for its softness, warmth, and hypoallergenic properties.

Are alpacas good for small farms?

Answer: Yes, alpacas are suitable for small farms due to their relatively low space requirements and gentle nature. They can be a good choice for hobby farms and small-scale fiber production.

CONCLUSION

Alpaca farming, a growing and dynamic industry, offers a unique blend of environmental sustainability, economic opportunity, and personal fulfillment. As the global interest in eco-friendly practices and natural fibers intensifies, alpaca farming emerges as a viable and appealing option for both small-scale and commercial agriculture.

One of the primary benefits of alpaca farming is its minimal environmental impact. Alpacas are gentle grazers that cause less damage to pastures compared to other livestock. Their unique padded feet minimize soil erosion, and their low methane emissions make them a more environmentally friendly choice. The animals produce high-quality fiber that is biodegradable and requires less water and energy to process compared to synthetic fibers.

This aligns well with the growing consumer demand for sustainable and eco-conscious products.

Economically, alpaca farming can be highly rewarding. Alpacas are relatively low-maintenance animals with a long lifespan, which translates to a long-term investment. Their fiber, known for its softness, warmth, and hypoallergenic properties, is highly prized in the textile industry, providing farmers with a lucrative revenue stream. Additionally, alpaca breeding can be a profitable venture, with quality breeding stock often commanding high prices. Farmers can diversify their income by offering tours, educational programs, and workshops, further enhancing the economic viability of their operations.

The personal satisfaction derived from alpaca farming cannot be overstated. Many farmers find joy in their daily care and interaction with their animals. Alpacas are known for their gentle and curious nature, making them enjoyable companions and creating a serene farming experience. The process of raising and breeding alpacas fosters a deep connection to the land and the animals, providing a sense of purpose and achievement.

Despite these advantages, successful alpaca farming requires careful planning and management. Prospective farmers must be prepared for initial investments in infrastructure and education. Understanding the specific needs of alpacas, including their nutritional requirements and health care, is crucial. Additionally, building a network with other alpaca breeders and participating in industry associations can provide valuable support and knowledge.

In conclusion, alpaca farming presents a compelling opportunity for those interested in sustainable agriculture, economic potential, and personal fulfillment. With its environmental benefits, economic rewards, and the joy of working with these charming animals, alpaca farming stands out as a rewarding venture for the modern farmer. As the industry continues to evolve, it holds promise for a thriving and sustainable future.

THE END

www.ingramcontent.com/pod-product-compliance
Lightning Source LLC
Chambersburg PA
CBHW071836210526
45479CB00001B/156